BEASTIES IN MY BACKYARD

Written by Camilla de la Bédoyère

Editors: Sarah Eason and Jennifer Sanderson

Designers: Paul Myerscough and Geoff Ward

Art Director: Susi Martin

Editorial Director: Laura Knowles

Publisher: Zeta Jones

Copyright © Marshall Editions 2016
Part of The Quarto Group
The Old Brewery, 6 Blundell Street,
London, N7 9BH

First published in the UK in 2016 by QED Publishing

ISBN 978-1-78493-436-1
Printed in China

10 9 8 7 6 5 4 3 2 1

BEASTIES IN MY BACKYARD

CAMILLA DE LA BÉDOYÈRE

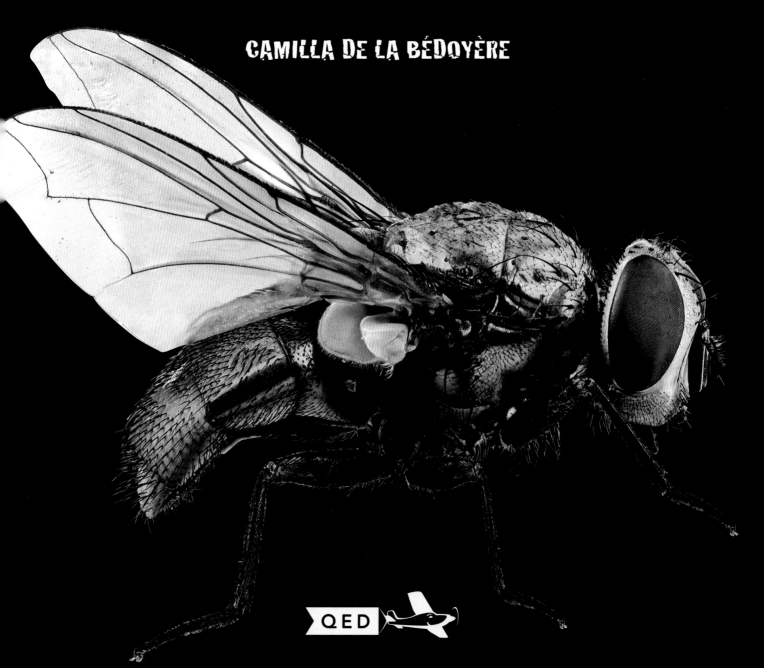

QED

CONTENTS

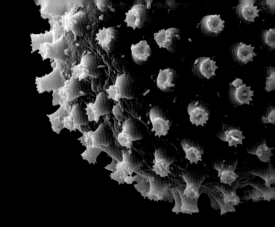

BEASTS BENEATH YOUR FEET

Gardens are packed with life. Stand still and use your eyes and ears to discover some of the many animals that make their homes in backyards, parks, gardens and wasteland. The most fascinating of these creatures are the invertebrates – small animals that do not have backbones.

⊕ HABITATS ARE HOMES

Habitats are places where animals or plants live. A garden is a habitat, but so is the soil inside a plant pot, a compost bin or the cracks in a tree's bark. A garden is packed with these 'microhabitats'.

*Many adult insects have **compound eyes**, made up of lots of tiny lenses. They are so big, the bug can see all around.*

Exoskeleton
Invertebrates do not have bones to support their bodies, which is why they cannot grow very big. Many of them have a tough skin, called an exoskeleton, instead. Exoskeletons can be colourful and patterned.

⊕ LIFE CYCLES

The story of how an animal grows from an egg into an adult that lays eggs is called a life cycle. Young insects are called larvae or nymphs. Many look very different from the adults they will become.

Body parts
Invertebrate bodies are divided into sections, or parts. Insects have three sections: a head, a thorax and an abdomen.

Sense organs
Invertebrates use their senses to find out about the world. Like humans, they can see, smell, touch, taste and hear, but some of their senses are far better than ours. The sensitive feelers on their heads are called antennae.

Legs
Most invertebrates have legs. Insects have three pairs of legs, and spiders have four pairs of legs.

The invertebrates you are most likely to find in the garden will be:
- Arachnids (spiders, mites, ticks and scorpions)
- Insects (flies, butterflies, bees, beetles and ants)
- Molluscs and annelids (slugs and snails, and worms)
- Centipedes, millipedes, woodlice

WATER BEARS

Water bears are so small that most people do not even know they exist. These invertebrates belong to a group of about 1000 species of animal called tardigrades. They are among the toughest and smallest creatures alive. Water bears have been on the planet for about 500 million years.

TOUGH BEASTS

Water bears prefer to live in damp or wet places. They can squeeze between particles of sand or soil in a garden, and they can also survive in rivers and oceans. They can live in extreme conditions and have been found in deserts and even in the soil under ice.

CLAWS

A water bear's feet are equipped with sharp, curved claws. The animal uses its claws to dig itself into a safe, damp habitat, such as moss or soil.

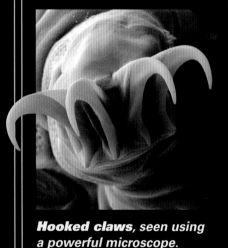

Hooked claws, seen using a powerful microscope.

Legs
There are four pairs of short legs. They are used for crawling, walking and swimming.

Repair
Scientists do not know how tardigrades survive extreme heat and cold, but they know that their bodies can quickly repair any damage.

⊕ SURVIVOR

When a tardigrade is caught up in freezing temperatures or a drought, it can lose around 97 per cent of the water in its body. When this happens, some species produce a sugar to protect their cell walls from damage.

SPACE BEARS

Water bears and other microscopic organisms were sent into space to test their survival in extreme conditions. In space, the water bears dehydrated but they were rehydrated when they returned to Earth. Some of those that returned to Earth laid eggs.

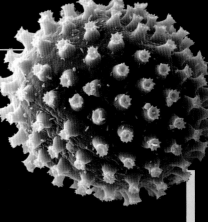

This water bear's egg was laid in damp moss.

Piglike
Water bears are also known as moss piglets because they often live in moss and they look quite like little pigs!

FACT FILE

TYPE
Class: Phylum
Order: Tardigrada

DIET
Plants and small animals

FOUND
Worldwide, including land, sea and fresh water

0 2 mm

SIZE • 0.3–1.2 MM

Stylets
Instead of teeth, water bears have hard, sharp stylets, which can pierce plant cells and small animals.

Tun
A water bear can survive some extreme conditions by turning itself into a 'tun'. It pulls its head and claws into its body, and dries out.

LIVING IN EXTREMES

Water bears can survive briefly in temperatures as hot as 125 degrees Celsius and as cold as -272 degrees Celsius.

GARDEN SNAILS

The common garden snail is a type of land snail. Most members of the snail's family – the molluscs – live in water. Garden snails are often seen as pests because they eat healthy plants. A large garden snail can leave a beautiful pot plant in shreds after just one night of feasting.

⊕ ON THE MOVE

When a snail moves, the muscles in its foot contract in waves, and it slides over the ground. Snails move out of their hiding places in the cool evenings and at night. During the day, they hide under rocks or leaves. In winter, garden snails hibernate to avoid freezing in the cold weather.

Shell
The snail's body makes its colourful shell for protection. The snail cannot separate itself from its shell because the shell is like hard skin.

SLIME

As the mollusc slithers forwards, it leaves a tell-tale trail of mucus, or slime. The slime helps the snail or slug to move smoothly across plants, rocks and other garden obstacles. The mucus is produced by a gland in the mollusc's foot and varies depending on the season and what the snail has eaten.

Slime *helps a snail to move and to stick to surfaces.*

⊕ WIDESPREAD

This species of land snail is originally from Europe, but over time, it has spread to parts of Asia, North America and Africa. Garden snails are edible, which means that humans can safely eat them. In some countries, the snails are farmed for food or for their slime, which is sometimes used in cosmetics.

Slugs and snails may be pests in the garden, but they are important food for other visitors, such as birds, frogs, newts, toads and lizards.

SLUGS

Slugs are closely related to snails, but they do not grow a protective shell. Slugs are rarely seen in the daytime because they dry out quickly in the sunshine. At night, they come out to eat garden plants.

Leopard slugs grow to about 12 centimetres long.

Tentacles
The head has two pairs of tentacles. There is an eye on the tip of each of the two largest tentacles.

Moist skin
The skin is protected from sharp stones and from drying out by a thick mucus.

Foot
The muscular part of a mollusc's body is called its foot. The mollusc uses it to move.

FACT FILE

TYPE
Class: Gastropoda
Order: Pulmonata

DIET
Plants

FOUND
Worldwide, in damp or cool habitats

0   2 cm

SIZE • 2–4 CM (SHELL WIDTH)

COMMON EARTHWORMS

Healthy garden soil is home to many earthworms. These slender invertebrates help to keep the soil fertile by burrowing through it and eating it. During the day, they burrow underground, and after rain or at night, they slither to the surface.

SEGMENTS

An earthworm's long body is made up of many parts, or segments. Each segment is called an annulus. Together, they give the body a cylinder shape. When a worm moves, its body stretches and can reach 35 centimetres long.

Each annulus contains muscles.

Skin
Worms breathe through their damp skin.

Gut
A large gut runs through the centre of the worm's body, from its mouth to its anus.

Earthworms and their relatives are food for birds, frogs, lizards and other animals, such as this mole.

SOIL EATERS

Earthworms eat fallen leaves and rotting plant material, such as roots. As they burrow, they eat soil, and their gut removes nutrients from it. Earthworms can eat about one-third of their body weight in soil every day.

BRISTLES

There are pairs of bristles along the length of the body. They are hooklike and grip to move the worm forward as it slithers.

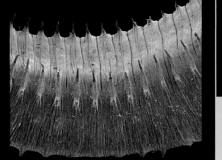

These tiny bristles are called 'setae'.

HEALTHY SOIL

When an earthworm burrows, it creates tunnels in the soil. The tunnels allow oxygen to pass through and keep the soil healthy. The waste that passes out of earthworms' bodies also helps plants to grow.

Clitellum
This area is called a clitellum. It is used when the earthworm mates.

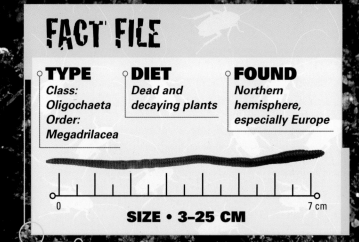

FACT FILE

TYPE	DIET	FOUND
Class: Oligochaeta Order: Megadrilacea	Dead and decaying plants	Northern hemisphere, especially Europe

0   7 cm

SIZE • 3–25 CM

CENTIPEDES

The name 'centipede' means '100 feet'. These common invertebrates can run very fast, but do not really have that many feet. House centipedes, unlike millipedes, hunt other animals to eat. They use venomous (poisonous) claws to sting their prey but they are mostly harmless to humans.

There are venomous claws by the broad, flat head. The antennae are long and can have up to 80 segments. The antennae sense smell, touch, vibrations and taste.

FACT FILE

TYPE
Class: Chilopoda
Order: Lithobiomorpha

DIET
Insects and spiders

FOUND
Worldwide in cool, damp places, especially Europe

0   30 mm

SIZE • 24–35 MM

✦ GROWING UP

Some female centipedes look after their eggs until they hatch. When little centipedes hatch, they have just seven pairs of legs, but they develop new legs as they grow bigger. Centipedes always have an odd number of leg pairs – this is why they never have exactly 100 legs.

Segments
Centipedes are arthropods, with a tough exoskeleton and a body divided into segments. The body is long, thin and slightly flattened.

GIANT CENTIPEDES

There are about 3150 species of centipede. Giant centipedes live in rainforests around the world. They feed on frogs, spiders, birds, lizards, rodents and even bats. Like all centipedes, they have claws that curve around their head, to inject venom into their prey.

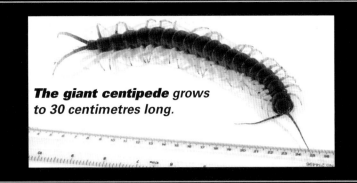

The giant centipede grows to 30 centimetres long.

GARDEN AND HOUSE

During hot summer months, centipedes prefer to hide underneath plant pots, in the soil or in any dark, cool and damp place in the garden. However, as summer fades, they often move into the warmth of a house to avoid the cold winter.

MILLIPEDES

Millipedes are similar to centipedes but they eat plants and usually have two pairs of legs on each body segment. There are about 10,000 species of millipede. Unlike centipedes, when millipedes feel threatened, they roll themselves into a coil.

A millipede's exoskeleton protects it, like armour.

Antennae-like legs
The last set of legs look like antennae, making it difficult to tell which is the head end.

DRAGONFLIES

Dragonflies visit gardens on warm sunny days, especially if there is water nearby and there are plenty of other insects to eat. These are fast fliers with superb hunting skills and eyesight. Each eye is made up of about 28,000 lenses, and dragonflies can probably see far more colours and detail than humans can.

Huge eyes
The eyes take up most of the insect's head, allowing it to see in almost all directions at once. They are made up of many lenses, and are called compound eyes.

LIFE CYCLE

When adult dragonflies emerge from a pond, they must hunt for food and find a mate. Females lay eggs in water, where they will develop into nymphs. When the adult is ready to emerge, it climbs up a plant stem and sheds its old skin. Adult dragonflies are among the largest insects and have existed for at least 250 million years. This makes them one of the oldest groups of flying animals.

Nymphs can live for up to four years in water.

NYMPHS
Young dragonflies are called nymphs. They live in fresh water and hunt other animals, including tadpoles and fish.

Abdomen
Dragonflies have very long abdomens. The wings and legs are attached to the smaller thorax.

Wings
There are two pairs of large, powerful wings. They look delicate, but dragonflies can fly even in a strong wind.

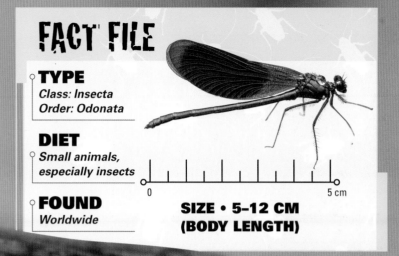

FACT FILE

TYPE
Class: Insecta
Order: Odonata

DIET
Small animals, especially insects

FOUND
Worldwide

0   5 cm
SIZE • 5–12 CM
(BODY LENGTH)

UNDER THE MICROSCOPE
Ridges on the surface of the wings help dragonflies to catch even small gusts of wind and lift the insects into the air.

*Like a scaffold, **struts** give wings strength.*

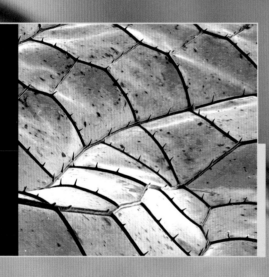

Like many animals, dragonflies bask in the sun to warm their bodies. They can move faster when they are warm.

DAMSELFLIES
There are more than 4000 species of dragonfly in the world today. Dragonflies belong to the same order of insects as damselflies, which are slightly smaller and more slender than dragonflies. Dragonflies usually rest with their wings held out, while damselflies tuck their wings close to their bodies when they settle.

GRASSHOPPERS

Short antennae
Two short and sensitive antennae grow from the head. They are used for touch and to smell.

A grasshopper may be difficult to see until it is startled and leaps to safety. Birds, snakes, lizards and frogs often prey on these insects, so their fast reactions help them to survive. There are more than 10,000 species of grasshopper.

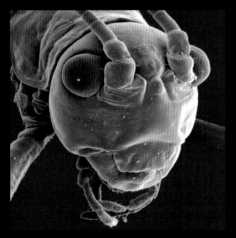

The palps can be seen just below the mouth.

Munching mouthparts
Grasshoppers are herbivores and their mouthparts are perfect for slicing and chewing tough grass.

SENSES
Grasshoppers have three simple eyes and two compound eyes that detect light and dark. There are two sensitive palps in front of the jaws, as well as antennae. Grasshoppers hear sounds using a drumlike organ – the tympanal organ – which is on their body, not their head.

Many grasshoppers are brown or green so they are well-camouflaged, but others are brightly coloured to warn predators that they taste foul.

FACT FILE

TYPE
Class: Insecta
Order: Orthoptera

DIET
Plants

FOUND
Worldwide, especially in grasslands

0   3 cm

SIZE • 1–8 CM

⊕ MAKING MUSIC

Male grasshoppers sing to attract females at mating time. They sing by rubbing their hind legs over a ridge on their wings, and females are attracted by the sound of their chirps. Females lay eggs in the soil or in plants. When the nymphs hatch, they have soft, pale bodies that quickly harden and darken in colour. Nymphs look like adult grasshoppers, but they do not have wings.

⊕ JUMPERS

The long hind (back) legs of a grasshopper have large, strong muscles and a 'spring' mechanism. The spring enables the legs to work like a catapult, thrusting the grasshopper forwards and upwards. A large grasshopper can leap one metre forwards and 25 centimetres upwards.

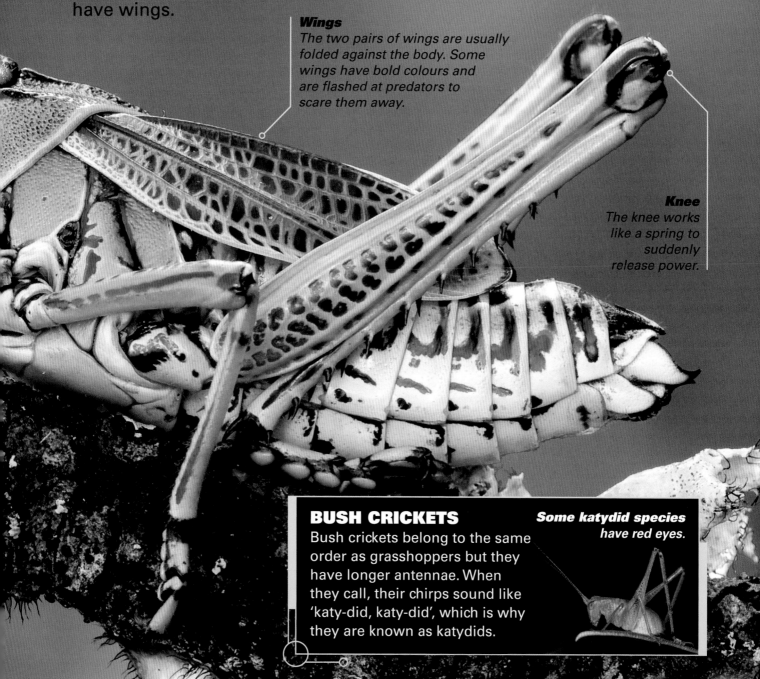

Wings
The two pairs of wings are usually folded against the body. Some wings have bold colours and are flashed at predators to scare them away.

Knee
The knee works like a spring to suddenly release power.

BUSH CRICKETS

Some katydid species have red eyes.

Bush crickets belong to the same order as grasshoppers but they have longer antennae. When they call, their chirps sound like 'katy-did, katy-did', which is why they are known as katydids.

EARWIGS

Earwigs are common garden bugs. They often hide beneath plant pots, where they stay during the day. They come out at night to hunt or search for food. There are about 2000 species of earwig and they are found throughout the world, especially in woodlands.

HUNTERS

Earwigs are scavengers, which means they eat old or rotting plant and animal matter. They sometimes hunt and eat other small animals, using their pincer-like cerci to grab hold of their prey. Gardeners often consider earwigs to be a pest because they also feed on flowers and vegetables.

A mother tends her young, keeping them safe.

GOOD MOTHERS

Few insects look after their eggs, but earwig mothers do. They sometimes care for their young, too. Young earwigs are called nymphs. They look similar to the adults.

The hind wings are big and fan-shaped, but earwigs usually walk and do not fly.

DEFENCE

Earwigs cannot bite hard. Instead, some types of earwig defend themselves by spraying a smelly liquid from the abdomen at attackers. This liquid covers a distance of 10 centimetres.

Earwigs have simple mouthparts.

Cerci
There is a pair of pincer-like cerci at the end of the insect's abdomen. They are straight in females and curved in males.

Body shape
An earwig's slender, flattened body is the right shape for squeezing between rocks, beneath plant pots or into the soil. Earwigs spend winter in these places.

Wings
Tough, leathery forewings cover and protect the delicate hind wings beneath.

MOULTING

Common earwigs lay their eggs in spring. The young that hatch must grow and moult their skin several times before they become adult earwigs. When an insect moults, it sheds old skin to reveal a new layer of skin beneath. In between moults, the young earwigs are called instars. They must leave their mother after they become the second instar, or she might eat them!

FACT FILE

TYPE
Class: Insecta
Order: Dermaptera

DIET
Plants and small animals

FOUND
Worldwide, especially woodlands

0				3 cm

SIZE • 1–5 CM

STICK INSECTS

Although stick insects are common in tropical forests, they also live in gardens in warm parts of the world. However, they can be very difficult to find. These bugs have one of the most impressive forms of camouflage in the animal world.

Wingless
Male stick insects sometimes have wings, but most females are wingless.

⊕ CAMOUFLAGE

There are about 2500 species of stick insect. They are also called walking sticks because they are long and sticklike, and perfectly shaped to hide among the twiggy parts of trees and bushes. Although they can stay perfectly still for hours, some types of stick insect sway from side to side instead, so they look like twigs that are moving in a gentle breeze.

Defence
Stick insects can lose a leg if they are attacked. However, young stick insects can grow a new one! Some stick insects produce foul liquids to scare away any predators.

LEAF INSECTS

Like stick insects, leaf insects also belong to the order Phasmatodea. There are about 30 species of leaf insects and they are mostly found in the forests of South East Asia and Australia. They are perfectly camouflaged for a life in trees or bushes, and they can sway in the breeze to complete the deception. Leaf insects have two sets of wings but use just one set to fly. When a leaf insect is resting, its wings are hidden from view.

Leaf insects are 3–11 centimetres long.

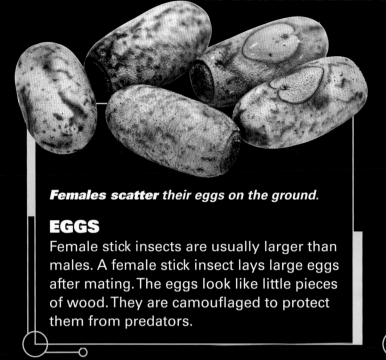

Females scatter their eggs on the ground.

EGGS

Female stick insects are usually larger than males. A female stick insect lays large eggs after mating. The eggs look like little pieces of wood. They are camouflaged to protect them from predators.

FACT FILE

TYPE
Class: Insecta
Order: Phasmatodea

DIET
Plants

FOUND
Worldwide, in warm places

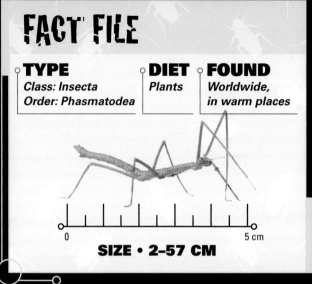

0   5 cm

SIZE • 2–57 CM

Mimicry
The way that a stick insect pretends to be a stick is called mimicry.

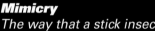

Long Body
Some species are more than 50 centimetres long, making them the longest known insects. Chan's megastick is the largest species – one measured 56.7 centimetres.

The goliath stick insect can grow to 25 centimetres long and it has large wings. This giant bug lives in Australian forests and gardens. It favours eucalyptus trees, which are indigenous (native) to Australia.

Legs
Stick insects' legs are long, ridged and sometimes spiky. The forelegs can be held in front of the head.

PRAYING MANTISES

Mantises are some of the world's most incredible predators. They may be small, but these bugs are fearless hunters with lightning-quick reactions and lethal weapons: powerful jaws and slashing, grabbing claws. They are impressive killers. The females even turn on males, and eat them.

Flower mantises can mimic petals, buds and leaves.

SPINY FLOWER MANTIS

Flower mantises mimic flowers. This helps them to be perfectly camouflaged as they lie in wait for bugs to come near.

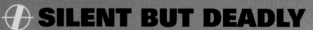 **SILENT BUT DEADLY**

Like many other bug predators, mantises lie in wait for their prey. They remain motionless on a plant until another insect comes close. Then, they whip their spiked forelimbs forwards and grab the prey. Mantises eat their prey alive.

Small head
The head is small, but the compound eyes are large and face forwards. They are perfect for seeing prey clearly.

Long antennae
The two sensitive antennae are long and thin.

Turning head
Mantises can turn their heads around to see what is happening behind them, and escape if a predator is nearby.

⊕ PRAYING POSE

Mantises are described as 'praying' because they hold up their forelimbs, as if they are in prayer. Mantis's legs and wings are long and slender. Some species do not have wings. There are more than 2000 different kinds of mantises, including European mantises and flower mantises.

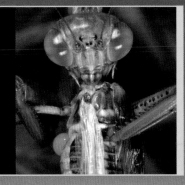
An insect's chewing mouthparts are called **mandibles**. A mantis's mouthparts are tough enough to chew beetles and scorpions.

FACT FILE

TYPE
Class: Insecta
Order: Mantodea

DIET
Small animals, mainly insects and spiders

FOUND
Worldwide, in warm places

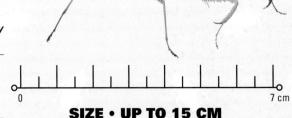

0   7 cm

SIZE • UP TO 15 CM

Green or brown
The tough outer skin, called the exoskeleton, is usually green or brown, but mantises can even be pink. Their colour camouflages them when they are on plants.

COCKROACHES

Cockroaches are some of the world's most successful animals. They live in gardens, houses and woodlands, but they can also survive long periods of time in extreme conditions, with no food or water. There are about 4500 different kinds of cockroach, and some of those are household pests.

⊕ SCAVENGERS

Cockroaches do not hunt for prey. They are not fussy eaters and will devour almost anything they find, including rotting food, dead animals and plants. Cockroaches easily pick up bacteria on their feet when they feed, and can spread diseases, such as Salmonella. Salmonella causes an infection of the intestines. Its symptoms in people include diarrhoea.

WARNING
Most cockroaches are dull brown, but some have bright yellow, red or orange markings. The vibrant colours warn predators that these species can release a foul-smelling liquid from their bodies.

Yellow and red are nature's warning colours.

Flat body
The body is flattened for squeezing into small, dark spaces. It has an oval shape.

Wings
Delicate hind wings, sometimes used for flying, are protected by tough, leathery forewings.

⊕ BABY BUGS

Female cockroaches produce up to 50 sticky egg cases in their life time, with each case containing 12–14 eggs. Some species carry the case on their abdomen until the eggs are ready to hatch. Others do not lay their eggs at all, but keep them inside their bodies and give birth to live young. The young are small and white, but they quickly grow. Cockroaches live for several months, up to two years.

Cockroaches have compound eyes and can see well in the dark. Their antennae are long and made up of many segments.

Pronotum
A shield-shaped body part covers the thorax and protects the head. It is called a pronotum.

FACT FILE

TYPE
Class: Insecta
Order: Blattodea

DIET
Plants, and anything else they find

FOUND
Worldwide, especially warm, dark places

0   30 mm

SIZE • 15–100 MM

BIG PESTS

American cockroaches are considered one of the biggest pest cockroaches and can grow to 4 centimetres in length.

These pests are common in city dumps and restaurants.

TERMITES

Termites are also known as 'white ants' but they are not actually ants. In fact, they are more closely related to cockroaches. Termites are described as 'social insects' because they live in large groups, called colonies, and share the work of looking after the young. There are about 3000 species of termite, but only about 300 of these are pests.

WOOD EATERS

These small insects make their home in soil or in wood. They eat plant material, which they are able to digest thanks to special bacteria in their guts. Termites help to break down dead and rotting woody plants. They can be a problem to people because they often damage garden sheds, fences and houses.

Exoskeleton
Soldier termites have thicker, stronger exoskeletons than worker termites, which often have pale, soft bodies.

Termite mounds stay cool and dry inside.

TERMITE MOUNDS
In tropical areas, termites can build huge mounds from soil, where they live. The tallest mounds can reach 6 metres tall.

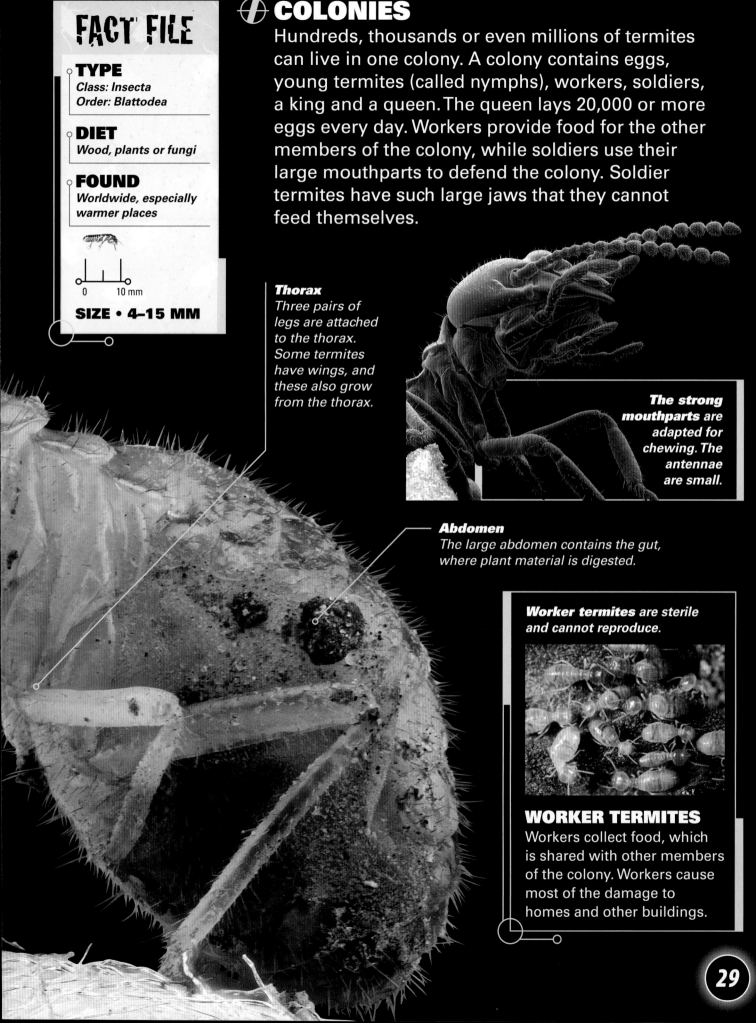

FACT FILE

TYPE
Class: Insecta
Order: Blattodea

DIET
Wood, plants or fungi

FOUND
Worldwide, especially warmer places

0   10 mm

SIZE • 4–15 MM

Hundreds, thousands or even millions of termites can live in one colony. A colony contains eggs, young termites (called nymphs), workers, soldiers, a king and a queen. The queen lays 20,000 or more eggs every day. Workers provide food for the other members of the colony, while soldiers use their large mouthparts to defend the colony. Soldier termites have such large jaws that they cannot feed themselves.

Thorax
Three pairs of legs are attached to the thorax. Some termites have wings, and these also grow from the thorax.

The strong mouthparts are adapted for chewing. The antennae are small.

Abdomen
The large abdomen contains the gut, where plant material is digested.

Worker termites are sterile and cannot reproduce.

WORKER TERMITES

Workers collect food, which is shared with other members of the colony. Workers cause most of the damage to homes and other buildings.

APHIDS

Aphids are small, flying insects that suck the sap from plants. This damages the plants and may stop them from growing well. Aphids are also known as whiteflies, greenflies and blackflies, depending on their colour. Aphids spread diseases between plants, so they are not a gardener's friend!

HONEYDEW

Aphids make a sugary liquid called honeydew. Ants like to eat honeydew, so they often take care of aphids, even carrying them from an unhealthy plant to another healthy one.

FLYING APHID

There are two pairs of wings, and the hind wings are smaller than the forewings. Not all aphids grow wings.

Body shape
An aphid's body is pear-shaped. A pair of tubes at the tip of the abdomen release a fluid that may deter predators from eating the insect.

There may be many aphids gathered on just one leaf or stem, which means they can cause a lot of damage in a short time.

Mouthparts
An aphid's mouthparts are the right shape for piercing a hole into a plant, and sucking out the sap inside it.

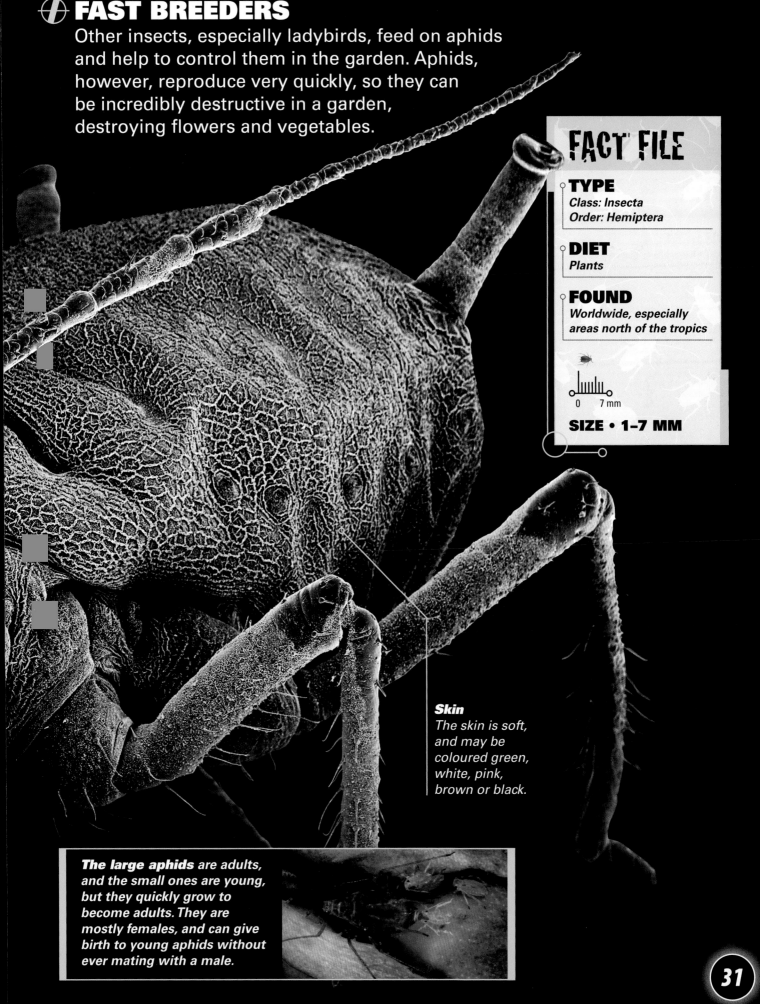

FAST BREEDERS

Other insects, especially ladybirds, feed on aphids and help to control them in the garden. Aphids, however, reproduce very quickly, so they can be incredibly destructive in a garden, destroying flowers and vegetables.

FACT FILE

TYPE
Class: Insecta
Order: Hemiptera

DIET
Plants

FOUND
Worldwide, especially areas north of the tropics

0   7 mm

SIZE • 1–7 MM

Skin
The skin is soft, and may be coloured green, white, pink, brown or black.

The large aphids are adults, and the small ones are young, but they quickly grow to become adults. They are mostly females, and can give birth to young aphids without ever mating with a male.

GIANT WATER BUGS

The eggs carried by their father are called a brood. He looks after his eggs because if they are not protected, they are more likely to be eaten by other animals.

Giant water bugs are related to aphids, termites and cicadas, but they live in fresh water. They are common in slow-moving streams, lakes and ponds. They are also known as electric light bugs and 'toe-biters' because they are attracted to electric lights, and sometimes they bite people. There are about 150 species of giant water bug.

⊕ HARD-WORKING FATHERS

Giant water bugs do something very unusual for an insect: the males take care of the eggs. The female giant water bug lays her eggs on the back of their father. He carries the eggs around until they are ready to hatch.

Body shape
The body is large and oval-shaped. Beneath the wings is a space in which the bug can trap a bubble of air to breathe underwater.

Water bugs can dive below the water surface.

SWIMMING LEGS

There are sharp claws on the front legs, and hairs on the two pairs of swimming legs. The hairs increase the surface area of the legs, making it easier for the bug to 'row' through the water.

HUNGRY BUGS

Giant water bugs have big appetites, and they have the power and weapons to attack and kill large prey. They mostly eat insects and other invertebrates, tadpoles and small fish, but some species attack baby turtles and small snakes.

Powerful legs
The front pair of legs has claws for catching prey.

Mouthparts
Their mouthparts work like a sharp beak to pierce through the skin of the bug's prey.

Muddy colour
The dull colour and body shape help the bug to mimic a dead leaf on the surface of the water. This makes it easier for a bug to ambush its prey and hide from predators such as birds and frogs.

FACT FILE

TYPE
Class: Insecta
Order: Hemiptera

DIET
Small animals

FOUND
Worldwide in fresh water

0   40 mm

SIZE • 15–100 MM

FROGHOPPERS

Froghoppers live on plants and are especially common in gardens, parks and meadows, where they feed on plants and plants' sap. They are superb jumpers and can leap out of danger when predators, such as birds, come too close.

Pronotum
The shield-shaped pronotum is larger than the head and helps to protect it.

BRIGHT COLOURS

Most froghoppers are green or brown but some types, such as this red-and-black froghopper, are brightly coloured. This species grows up to 11 millimetres long and is common in Europe.

This froghopper lives in grassy places like gardens.

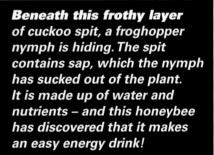

Beneath this frothy layer of cuckoo spit, a froghopper nymph is hiding. The spit contains sap, which the nymph has sucked out of the plant. It is made up of water and nutrients – and this honeybee has discovered that it makes an easy energy drink!

BUGS

Froghoppers belong to a group of insects that are called bugs (although the word 'bug' is also used to describe all sorts of creepy-crawlies). There are nearly 90,000 species of bug. They have two pairs of wings and mouthparts that are shaped for piercing and sucking. Many garden bugs are pests because they damage plants.

Folded wings
Most froghoppers hold their wings against their body, protecting the soft abdomen.

Legs
There are six pairs of legs. There are spines on the hind legs. Froghoppers can leap up to 70 centimetres in a single jump.

CUCKOO SPIT

Young froghoppers are called nymphs. The nymphs coat themselves in thick froth, which they make by pushing air bubbles into a liquid that comes out of the bugs' anus. This froth is called cuckoo spit. It covers a nymph and protects it from predators while it sucks plant sap. It also stops it from drying out in the sunshine.

UP CLOSE
Froghoppers have large, round eyes. The mouthparts of nymphs are perfect for sucking sap, but adults eat leaves and stems too.

Froghoppers are also called spittlebugs.

35

CICADAS

Cicadas can be heard long before they can be seen, especially when these bugs gather together in groups at mating time. Adult cicadas can fly and are common around trees and in gardens. Their nymphs, however, are harder to see, as they live underground where they feed on roots.

NOISY BUGS

Male cicadas are the loudest insects with 'songs'. They can be heard 400 metres away. Their songs are so loud that when they sing together, the noise can be painful to the human ear. Males 'sing' by vibrating a membrane on their abdomen so fast that it creates pulses of sound, which are amplified (made louder) by a space beneath. Males sing to attract females at mating time.

Body shape
The body is large, heavy and oval-shaped. There are two pairs of wings that are folded back against the body.

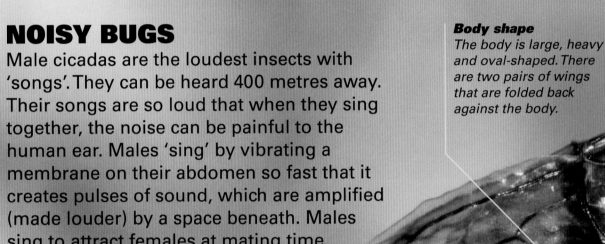

Cicadas are heavy bugs, and noisy flyers.

FLYING
The forewings are longer than the hind wings and they are usually transparent (see-through), or have some markings for camouflage.

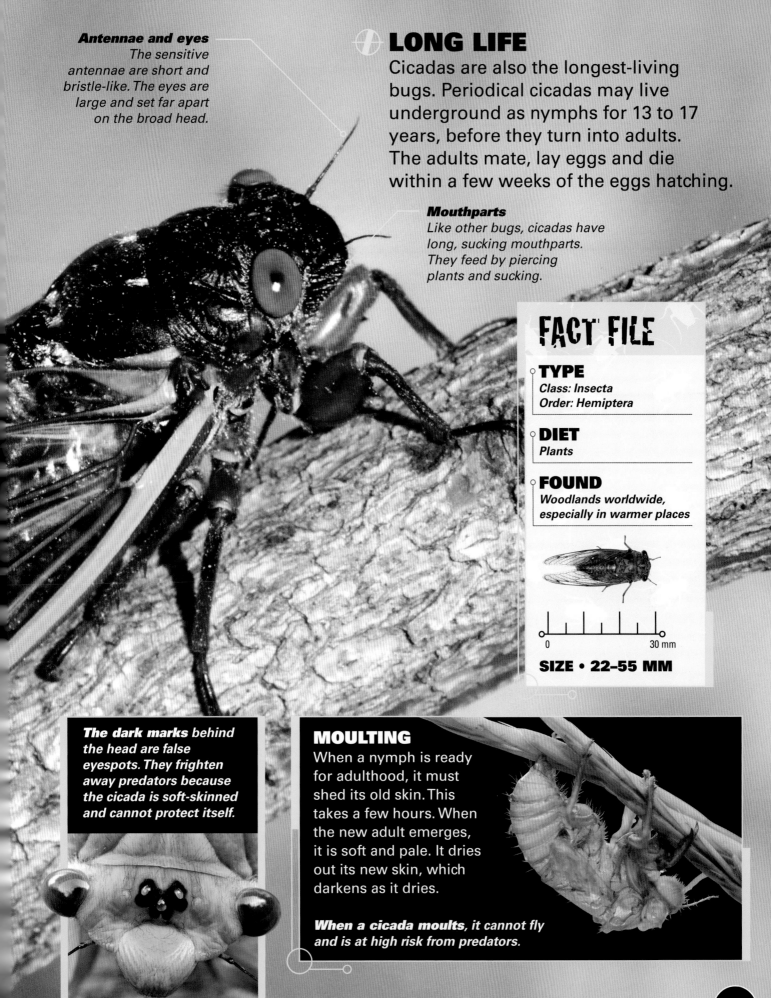

Antennae and eyes
The sensitive antennae are short and bristle-like. The eyes are large and set far apart on the broad head.

LONG LIFE

Cicadas are also the longest-living bugs. Periodical cicadas may live underground as nymphs for 13 to 17 years, before they turn into adults. The adults mate, lay eggs and die within a few weeks of the eggs hatching.

Mouthparts
Like other bugs, cicadas have long, sucking mouthparts. They feed by piercing plants and sucking.

FACT FILE

TYPE
Class: Insecta
Order: Hemiptera

DIET
Plants

FOUND
Woodlands worldwide, especially in warmer places

0   30 mm

SIZE • 22–55 MM

The dark marks behind the head are false eyespots. They frighten away predators because the cicada is soft-skinned and cannot protect itself.

MOULTING

When a nymph is ready for adulthood, it must shed its old skin. This takes a few hours. When the new adult emerges, it is soft and pale. It dries out its new skin, which darkens as it dries.

When a cicada moults, it cannot fly and is at high risk from predators.

POND SKATERS

A garden pond may seem peaceful and motionless, until you get close and look carefully at its surface. Groups of pond skaters scoot across the water, using their legs to sense any movement, which signals that food – in the form of other insects – is nearby.

 ## WATER STRIDERS

Pond skaters are also known as water striders. They use their long, thin legs to spread their weight over water so they can skate along its surface without sinking. Most of the movement is made by the middle pair of legs, which work together like a pair of oars.

Wings
Like all members of the bug family, pond skaters have two pairs of wings. They can fly to a new pond if their own pond becomes too crowded with other pond skaters.

Legs
The forelegs are short and used for catching prey, or grabbing hold of dead insects. The hind legs are used like rudders, to steer the insect as it skates.

PREDATORS

Pond skaters are predators that feed on other insects. They grab them with claws and stab them with piercing mouthparts. They also feed on dead insects and spiders that they find.

As it scoots across the pond, a pond skater searches for food.

⊕ SURVIVAL

Pond skaters must leap to escape hungry predators, such as birds. They can survive cold winters, when ponds freeze over, by hibernating. They emerge from hibernation in spring, to mate and lay their eggs.

Dark bodies
There are at least 750 species of pond skater. Their dark bodies are covered in hairs.

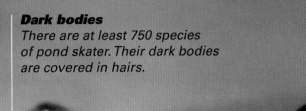

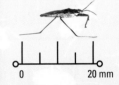
The front legs on a pond skater's body help it to sense any vibrations on the water surface. The legs have hairs that repel water, so the insect can stay dry.

NYMPHS

Pond skater nymphs hatch from eggs and moult several times before they are adults. Between the moults, they go through five stages, known as instars. Adults sometimes eat the nymphs.

Instars can also skate across the water's surface.

SHIELD BUGS

Shield bugs are sometimes called stink bugs because they are able to make foul smells. There are at least 5500 species of shield bug. Most species use their sucking mouthparts to feed on plants, often damaging them – especially if many shield bugs gather on one plant. However, some shield bugs are predators and attack caterpillars.

⊕ TOXIC SHOCK

Any bird that tries to eat a shield bug gets a nasty shock when the bug releases foul-smelling liquids from between its first and second pairs of legs. The smell is similar to that of mouldy almonds, so humans do not usually find it disgusting. In some countries, stink bugs are cooked and eaten.

Red shield bugs do not need to hide from predators.

FOUL TASTE

These bugs have clever ways to stay alive. Some are coloured to warn predators to stay away. Bold colours, especially red and yellow, suggest that an insect tastes bad, or has a stinger, so these bugs are often left alone. Shield bugs survive the cold winter weather by hibernating.

FACT FILE

TYPE
Class: Insecta
Order: Hemiptera

DIET
Mostly plants, although some hunt as adults

FOUND
Worldwide

0   15 mm

SIZE • 5–25 MM

HUNGRY NYMPHS

When the nymphs hatch from their eggs, they eat their egg cases, which their mother has coated with bacteria. The nymphs need the bacteria in their guts to digest the plant sap they will eat. Nymphs look like adults and they can also make a stink to defend themselves.

The newly laid eggs stick to the surface of a leaf.

TAKING CARE

Females can lay up to 400 eggs in their lifetime. Unlike most insects, shield bug mothers guard their eggs from predators. Some species sit on their eggs, like a bird hatching its brood. When they hatch, the nymphs feed on the plant they are on, but some become predators.

Pronotum
The pronotum – the first segment of the thorax – is large and may have square edges.

Wings
The forewings are thicker and stronger than the hind wings. They protect the softer hind wings, which are hidden beneath.

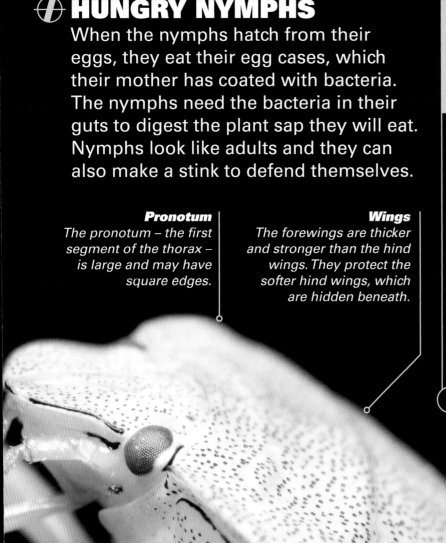

Body shape
The body is shaped like a shield, giving the shield bug its common name. Most shield bugs are green, so they are hard to see on a plant, unless they are basking in the sun.

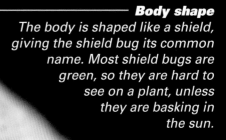

Firebugs are shield bugs with distinctive red and black markings, which also give them their other common name of clown-faced bug.

WOODLICE

These familiar bugs are not insects: they are crustaceans. Woodlice are closely related to animals that live in water, such as crabs, lobsters and shrimps. Woodlice are also known as sow bugs.

HABITAT

Although woodlice originally lived in Europe, they are now also found in North America and elsewhere around the world. They need damp, cool habitats, so they hide between rocks, in the soil, in piles of leaves and compost or under plant pots. Woodlice also squeeze into gaps beneath tree bark.

MOULTING

Like other arthropods, woodlice must shed their old skin as they grow. This is called moulting and they do it in two halves: they shed the back half first.

The old skin appears pale as it lifts off the body.

Legs
There are seven pairs of legs that are mostly protected beneath the body as the bug scuttles around. When a woodlouse is scared, it can almost glue its feet to the ground.

Segments
The body is oval-shaped and divided into segments that have 'armour-plating' for protection. Woodlice are dull coloured, usually grey or glossy black.

PILL BUGS
Pill bugs are woodlice that roll themselves up into a ball when they are disturbed. This may save them from being attacked and eaten by predators.

Pill bugs are also known as pill woodlice.

FACT FILE

TYPE
Class: Malacostraca
Order: Isopoda

DIET
Plants

FOUND
Worldwide in dark, damp places

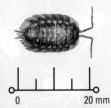

0   20 mm

SIZE • UP TO 18 MM

Antennae
The antennae look crooked and tap the ground as the woodlouse walks.

A mother keeps her eggs in a special pouch beneath her body until they are ready to hatch. The babies are small and white, but look similar to adults.

⊕ FOOD HABITS
Woodlice feed on dead plant matter, so they often make their homes in compost heaps, where they help to break down rotting leaves. They do not have good eyesight so they find their food by using their senses of touch and smell.

LADYBIRDS

These colourful beetles are some of the most popular garden beasties. Easy to recognize with their colourful bodies and patterns of spots and stripes, ladybirds eat garden pests, so it is no wonder that gardeners are pleased to see them. Ladybirds are also known as ladybugs or lady beetles.

SURVIVAL

A ladybird's bright, bold colours and patterns warn birds that it tastes bad. Some species of ladybird also produce a bad-smelling liquid – which looks like blood – from their joints. A bleeding, smelly insect is not appetizing, so the ladybird is left alone by a predator.

When a ladybird flies, it lifts its wing cases to reveal its flying wings.

IN FLIGHT

Ladybirds fly from plant to plant, looking for insects to eat – especially aphids. They are most active on warm, sunny days. In winter, they find a dark, safe place to stay.

Elytra
The glossy, hard forewings are called elytra. There are usually a number of spots decorating the elytra.

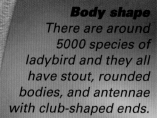

Body shape
There are around 5000 species of ladybird and they all have stout, rounded bodies, and antennae with club-shaped ends.

⊕ BEETLES

Ladybirds belong to an enormous group of insects called beetles: one in every three insects is a beetle! Beetles have wings. Their forewings are tough and often shiny. The forewings make a protective case over their more delicate hind wings, which are used for flying.

Pronotum
This body part is often black with white markings and shields the head, giving the beetle some protection from predators.

Harlequins are larger than most other ladybirds.

HARLEQUINS

Harlequin ladybirds are not popular with gardeners because they prey on other types of ladybird. They can also damage carpets and curtains if they settle inside a house. Harlequins have many different colours and patterns, and can have up to 21 orange-red or black spots.

Like other beetles, ladybird larvae look very different from the adults, and go through a process called pupation to become pupae. They then change from larvae to adults inside the pupae.

FACT FILE

TYPE
Class: Insecta
Order: Coleoptera

DIET
Mostly insects

FOUND
Worldwide

0   15 mm

SIZE • 1–15 MM

SCARAB BEETLES

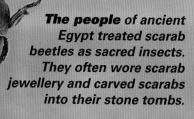

The people of ancient Egypt treated scarab beetles as sacred insects. They often wore scarab jewellery and carved scarabs into their stone tombs.

With at least 30,000 species, one of the largest groups of beetles is the scarab beetle group. The insects in this group live all over the world in many kinds of habitats, from parks and gardens to deserts and rainforests. This group includes some of the largest insects. The Hercules beetle can grow to 18 centimetres including its 'horns'.

Head shape
Some species have a simple head shape with chewing mandibles for eating plants. Others have large heads with horns for fighting, or they have shovel-shaped heads for moving plant material and dung.

Antennae
The sensitive antennae are often clubbed at the tips, or broad and fan-shaped.

BIG AND STRONG

Most scarab beetles in gardens and parks go about their business unnoticed. However, some scarab beetles are insect record breakers. The heaviest of all insects, for example, are the rhino beetles, which have giant larvae that weigh more than 200 grams. One species of dung beetle can lift more than 1100 times its own weight.

RHINO BEETLE
Rhino beetles are huge and strong. They are capable of lifting something 850 times heavier than themselves!

Males use their strange 'horns' to fight one another and to dig.

IN THE GARDEN

The larvae of many scarab beetles, such as chafers, feed on garden plants – especially grass roots. They are pests because they can do great damage. Others are welcome in the garden because they feed on old and rotting plant material, helping to return the nutrients to the soil, so more plants will grow.

A male fans out his antennae to pick up more scent.

HAIRY ANTENNAE

This European cockchafer is also known as a May bug or a June bug. 'Chafer' is an old word for 'chew'. The males have huge antennae, which they can use to smell females. They can smell females that are far away.

FACT FILE

TYPE
Class: Insecta
Order: Coleoptera

DIET
Varied

FOUND
Worldwide

0   30 mm

SIZE • 2–180 MM

DUNG BEETLES

Dung beetles collect faeces (dung) and lay their eggs inside, so their larvae can safely feed on it. They use the Sun and stars to help them find their way, as they move the dung to a safe place.

Dung beetles roll dung into balls so it is easy to move.

47

TIGER BEETLES

Tiger beetles belong to a huge group of beetles called ground beetles. There are about 30,000 species of ground beetle. Tiger beetles are found all over the world, in all types of habitat. Some tiger beetles live in trees, but most prefer to stay on the ground, especially in sandy, dry places.

⊕ RECORD BREAKER

Tiger beetles are the fastest-running insects in the world. The Australian tiger beetle holds the record for the fastest species, with a top speed of 9 kph. There are around 2000 species of tiger beetle.

Green tiger beetles live throughout Europe.

TYPES OF TIGER BEETLE

Tiger beetles are mostly very similar in size and shape, but while some are plain brown or black, others – such as this beautiful green tiger beetle – have a metallic shininess, called iridescence.

Colour
This is a blue-spotted tiger beetle, with shiny blue-green elytra (wing cases). Many tiger beetles are brightly coloured but some are dull.

Tiger beetles run so fast that they become blind while they are in pursuit. They must stop mid-run so they can get a good look before they set off again.

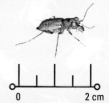
Big eyes
Most tiger beetles are nocturnal, so they need large eyes for spotting prey.

Body shape
The body is long and slender, and raised off the ground by three pairs of long legs. The three body parts (head, thorax and abdomen) are clearly separated.

FIERCE HUNTERS

Once a tiger beetle has caught up with its prey, it grabs hold of it and begins to crush it with massive, toothed jaws. It then pours its spit over its victim. The spit begins to dissolve the flesh, digesting it even before it is inside the beetle's guts.

With its large eyes, the beetle can see in all directions.

UP CLOSE

Seen up close, these beetles have a fearsome appearance. Their mandibles (grasping jaws) are large and curved. They can crunch prey easily.

STAG BEETLES

Stag beetles are easy to recognize. They have large, shiny bodies and huge mandibles that are used for fighting, rather than eating. As adults, they lumber along the ground, searching for mates. Stag beetles can fly, but they are cumbersome and noisy as they propel themselves slowly through the air.

FIGHTING

Males use their horns to grab one another and wrestle, fighting over mating space, or territory. Their huge heads are packed with muscles so they can push and shove their rivals. They usually emerge from pupation before the females, so when the females arrive, the winning males already have their mating space ready.

Body shape
The body is clearly separated into a head, thorax and abdomen. Most stag beetles are black, brown or red-brown. Some tropical species have iridescent exoskeletons.

ENDANGERED

There are about 1300 species of stag beetle and some of those, such as this European stag beetle, are endangered. Their habitats have been destroyed, and they are easy prey for large animals, such as cats and dogs, to kill.

Adult European stag beetles die before the winter sets in.

Giant jaws
The jaws of a stag beetle resemble the huge antlers of a male deer (or 'stag'), giving this group of insects their common name.

LIFE CYCLE

Eggs are laid in old trees or rotting wood. The large, white grubs can spend three years or more feeding on wood, before pupating inside a cocoon the size of an orange. They emerge as adults from spring to early summer. The adults do not usually feed, although they sometimes drink nectar from flowers or tree sap. Adult stag beetles die soon after the eggs are laid.

Antennae
The antennae come out from either side of the head, where they are less likely to get damaged during a fight.

Males have larger mandibles than females. However, the females are known to bite toes, giving a painful nip if they are disturbed.

FACT FILE

○ **TYPE**
Class: Insecta
Order: Coleoptera

○ **DIET**
Plants

○ **FOUND**
Worldwide

0   45 mm

SIZE • 5–90 MM

The giant larvae of stag beetles need to feed and grow undisturbed for a long time. Gardeners often leave piles of old wood in a corner of the garden so beetles can make a home for their larvae there.

CAT FLEAS

It is almost impossible to see cat fleas lurking in the backyard because they are tiny and hide out of sight. These mini-beasts prefer to live indoors, on a warm animal's body. However, sometimes fleas have to survive outdoors, waiting in dry, shady places for a pet cat or dog to pass by.

Fleas are able to scamper through fur because they are paper-thin. A slender body can pass between hairs easily and is difficult to squash.

⊕ THE HOST

Once a flea has sensed a warm-blooded animal nearby, it jumps aboard and nestles among the cat or dog's fur. Its unsuspecting host brings the flea into the home, and the flea soon starts to suck the pet's blood. This is when a female flea lays her eggs.

Legs
A flea's legs contain a rubbery material called resilin. This allows fleas to leap about 150 times their own length.

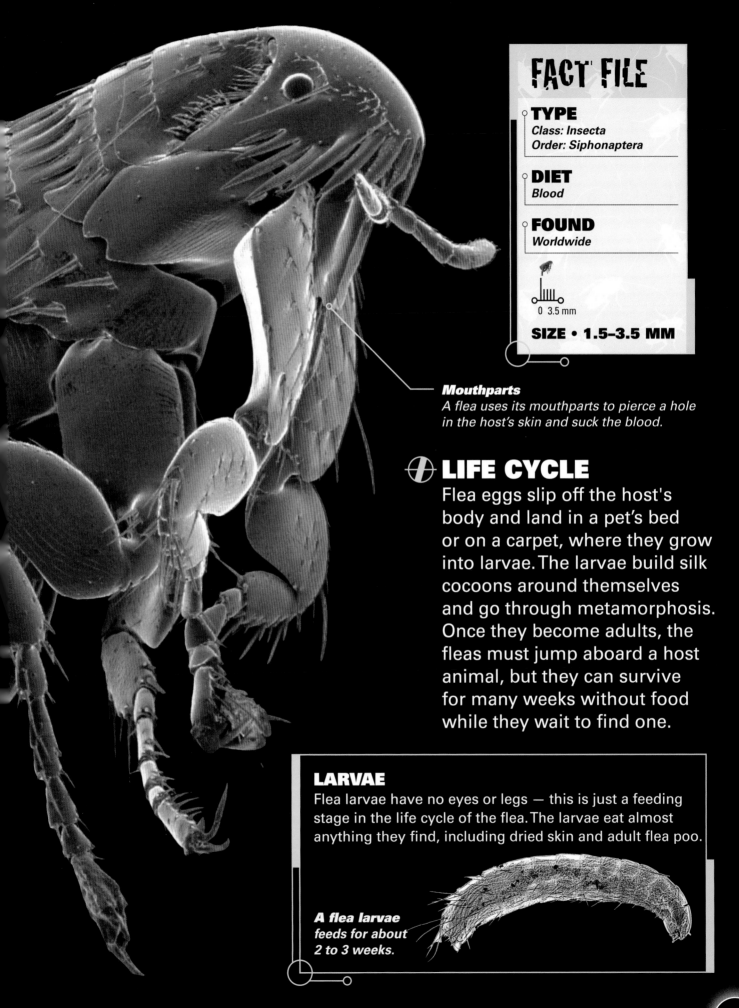

Mouthparts
A flea uses its mouthparts to pierce a hole in the host's skin and suck the blood.

⊕ LIFE CYCLE

Flea eggs slip off the host's body and land in a pet's bed or on a carpet, where they grow into larvae. The larvae build silk cocoons around themselves and go through metamorphosis. Once they become adults, the fleas must jump aboard a host animal, but they can survive for many weeks without food while they wait to find one.

LARVAE

Flea larvae have no eyes or legs — this is just a feeding stage in the life cycle of the flea. The larvae eat almost anything they find, including dried skin and adult flea poo.

A flea larvae feeds for about 2 to 3 weeks.

ROBBER FLIES

Robber flies love warm, sunny gardens where plenty of other little animals live. These insects are famous for their large appetites and hunting skills. There are more than 7000 species of robber fly.

PEST KILLERS

Robber flies fly quickly towards their prey, grabbing it and injecting it with toxic saliva (spit), using their proboscis to pierce the victim's body. The saliva stops the victim from moving and begins to dissolve its body, so the flies can suck up this liquid meal. Robber flies can suck out the insides of a bug in fewer than 30 minutes.

Wings
All insects in the order Diptera have just one pair of wings. Behind them, the hind wings have become a pair of balancing organs called halteres. Robber flies have broad wings.

Body shape
Some robber flies have large, stocky bodies, but others are slender and delicate. They are grey, black or brown.

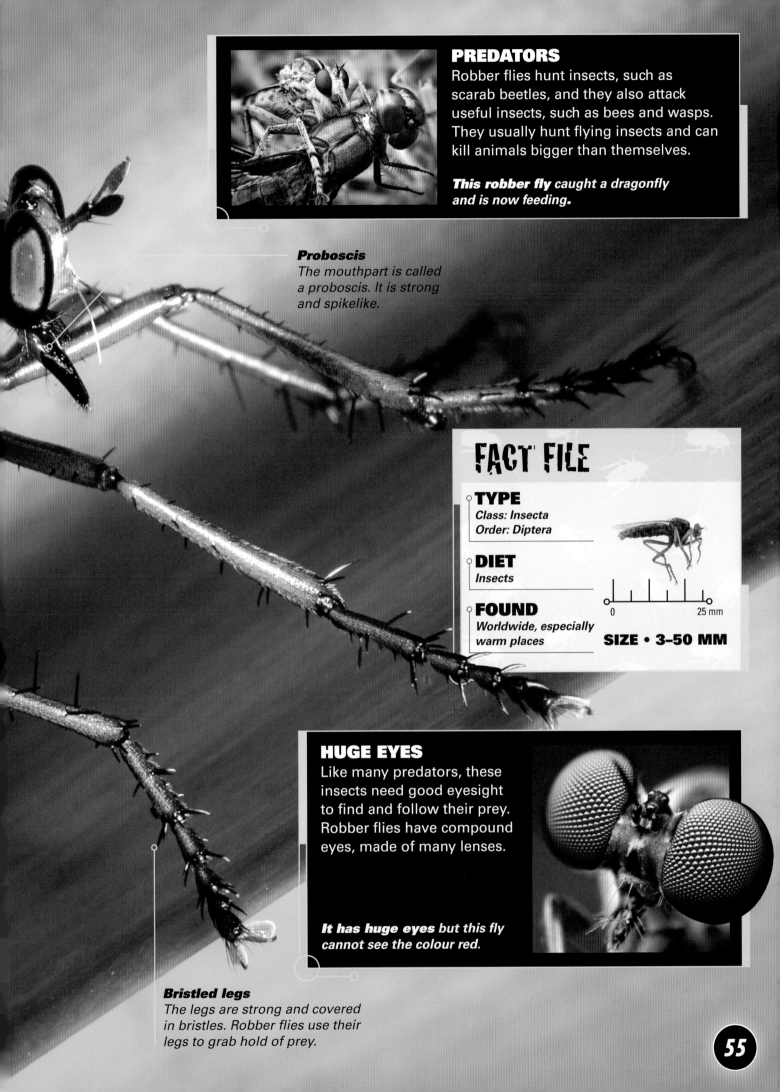

PREDATORS

Robber flies hunt insects, such as scarab beetles, and they also attack useful insects, such as bees and wasps. They usually hunt flying insects and can kill animals bigger than themselves.

This robber fly caught a dragonfly and is now feeding.

Proboscis
The mouthpart is called a proboscis. It is strong and spikelike.

FACT FILE

TYPE
Class: Insecta
Order: Diptera

DIET
Insects

FOUND
Worldwide, especially warm places

0   25 mm

SIZE • 3–50 MM

HUGE EYES

Like many predators, these insects need good eyesight to find and follow their prey. Robber flies have compound eyes, made of many lenses.

It has huge eyes but this fly cannot see the colour red.

Bristled legs
The legs are strong and covered in bristles. Robber flies use their legs to grab hold of prey.

BLOWFLIES

There are about 150,000 species of fly in the world and just 1500 of those are blowflies. Blowflies are a group of disease-spreading insects that are common in homes, parks and gardens. They are known as bluebottles and greenbottles because of the colour of their abdomens and thoraxes.

⊕ LIFE CYCLE

Adult females lay their eggs in rotting plants, food and animal bodies. The eggs hatch quickly and the small, white maggots feed on the food around them. When the flies are ready to turn into adults, they burrow into soil and pupate, building a protective brown shell around themselves as they metamorphose.

Thorax
The thorax is dark and has short spikes that are used to defend the fly from predators, such as birds and bats.

CLAWS

Like other flies, a blowfly is nimble on its feet and can walk on vertical surfaces, and can even walk upside down.

Blowflies have claws on their feet for gripping.

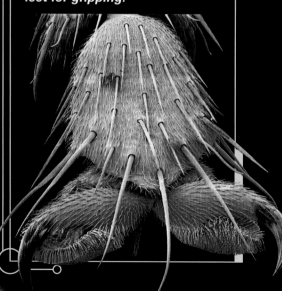

Antennae
The antennae are short and sensitive to strong smells, such as nectar or rotting animals.

Wings
There is just one pair of transparent wings. These insects are good flyers.

⊕ EATING HABITS

Some blowfly maggots prey on ants and other small invertebrates, while some adults burrow into the flesh of living animals to lay their eggs there, especially if they find a wound on the animal's skin. When the eggs hatch, just 12 hours later, the maggots start to feed on the flesh of the animal.

Adults suck up liquid using their spongelike mouthparts, and often feed on rotting food or fallen fruit.

Bristles
The plump body and the legs are covered with short bristles.

MOSQUITOES

Mosquitoes may be small, but they are one of the deadliest animals on the planet, spreading diseases such as malaria and dengue fever. These diseases infect humans, and malaria-spreading mosquitoes are found all over the world. Adult mosquitoes feed on blood and nectar.

FACT FILE

TYPE
Class: Insecta
Order: Diptera

DIET
Blood and nectar

FOUND
Worldwide, especially warm places

0   10 mm

SIZE • 3–20 MM

Abdomen
The flies are dull coloured but the abdomen of a female appears pink-red after it has eaten a blood meal.

HOUSE MOSQUITOES

The northern house mosquito is common in gardens and homes of North America. These insects suck blood from birds and humans or other mammals. They often spend winter inside houses.

Mosquitoes inject painkillers so victims do not feel the bite.

LIFE CYCLE

Only adult female mosquitoes drink blood. They need this food to lay their eggs. Eggs are placed in still or stagnant water, such as garden ponds, drains, buckets and watering cans. The larvae live in water and turn into pupae before emerging as flying adults.

58

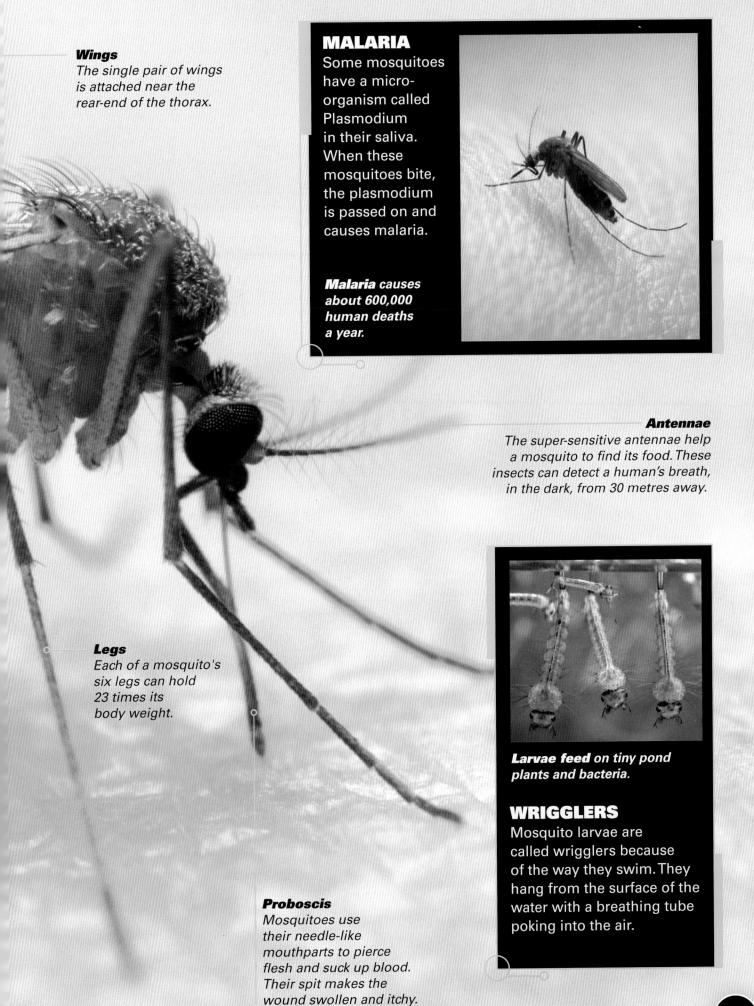

Wings
The single pair of wings is attached near the rear-end of the thorax.

MALARIA
Some mosquitoes have a micro-organism called Plasmodium in their saliva. When these mosquitoes bite, the plasmodium is passed on and causes malaria.

Malaria causes about 600,000 human deaths a year.

Antennae
The super-sensitive antennae help a mosquito to find its food. These insects can detect a human's breath, in the dark, from 30 metres away.

Legs
Each of a mosquito's six legs can hold 23 times its body weight.

Larvae feed on tiny pond plants and bacteria.

WRIGGLERS
Mosquito larvae are called wrigglers because of the way they swim. They hang from the surface of the water with a breathing tube poking into the air.

Proboscis
Mosquitoes use their needle-like mouthparts to pierce flesh and suck up blood. Their spit makes the wound swollen and itchy.

59

CRANE FLIES

With their long, gangly legs, crane flies deserve their other common name of daddy-long-legs. They belong to an old and successful group of insects, with about 15,000 species worldwide. Crane flies like damp habitats, and they are often found on damp garden lawns in the early morning.

Antennae
Each long antenna has 39 segments.

LEATHERJACKETS

Young crane flies are called leatherjackets. They are pests in a garden because they live in the soil, eating plant roots – especially grass roots. They can also live in water.

*This **leatherjacket** will become a pupa and then an adult.*

Mouthparts
The long mouthparts are called a rostrum. They are longer than the rest of the insect's head.

FAVOURITE FOOD

Crane flies are not fast flyers and they have no powerful way to protect themselves, such as a toxic bite or sting. They are a favourite food of other garden animals, especially birds, which poke around in soil looking for leatherjackets to eat.

BALANCING ACT

Most flying insects with long legs use their limbs to spread their weight on water or to feed, but crane flies probably use them to balance as they fly. They may also use their legs as 'feelers' to help them find their way in the dark and avoid bumping into things.

Long legs
Crane flies have extremely long legs. Although all crane flies should have six legs, it is common to see them with fewer because their legs are easily broken or shed.

Wings
There is one pair of long, transparent wings with distinct 'veins'. In the larger species, the wingspan can be up to 10 centimetres.

UP CLOSE
Seen up close, a crane fly's head looks extraordinary, with its huge eyes and long, beaklike mouthparts. Adults, however, rarely eat, and live for just a few weeks.

Crane flies have large compound eyes.

FACT FILE

TYPE
Class: Insecta
Order: Diptera

DIET
Plants and nectar

FOUND
Worldwide, especially damp habitats

0   30 mm

SIZE • 7–77 MM

Sometimes, crane flies drink a flower's nectar. When they fly between flowers, they carry pollen. This is called pollination and helps flowers to grow seeds.

LIGHTNING BUGS

Once the Sun has gone down, lightning bugs produce incredible flashes of light in trees. They are also known as fireflies or glow worms, but these insects are not worms, flies or bugs – they are beetles.

Larvae live for about one year.

LARVAE
Adults eat very little, but the larvae feed on invertebrates. The larvae also glow, and in some places they are called 'glow worms'. They look similar to the adults.

Wings
Males have wings, but some females are wingless.

MAKING LIGHT
These small nocturnal beetles have special places on their abdomens that make a cold, green light. At twilight, orange lights glow better, so some fireflies make orange light instead. The lights attract mates, and each species flashes its lights in a pattern that helps mates of its own species to find it.

Body shape
The body is a typical beetle shape, with an oval and exoskeleton. Most beetles have hard exoskeletons but lightning bugs have soft bodies.

Head
The head is hidden beneath a large, protective pronotum. The antennae are threadlike.

FACT FILE

TYPE
Class: Insecta
Order: Coleoptera

DIET
Nectar, pollen or invertebrates

FOUND
Worldwide, especially warm and wet places

0   15 mm

SIZE • 5–30 MM

Legs
There are three pairs of legs, each of which end in a single claw (double claws are more common in other beetles).

LIGHT ORGANS
The special places where light is made are called the light organs. They are on the underside of the fifth, sixth and seventh segments of the abdomen.

The green glow can be switched off and on.

TRICKERY
Some female lightning bugs flash lights in a way that is typical of other species, so curious males come close to investigate, with the hope of mating. In fact, the females lure them close just to eat them!

FUSSY FEMALES
Although both males and females can flash, males flash more, or brighter. Females prefer to mate with males who make the most flashes or the brightest lights.

Females must choose which male to mate with.

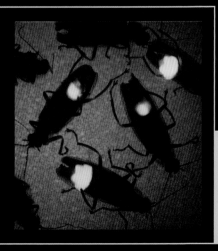

MONARCH BUTTERFLIES

There are more than 165,000 types of butterfly and moth, and many of them visit gardens. They lay their eggs on the leaves of plants – often called 'food plants' – where their larvae (caterpillars) will grow. Adults feed on nectar, which is the sweet liquid made by flowers to attract insects.

⊕ MIGRATION

Monarch butterflies are colourful insects that live in North America. They migrate to Mexico, where they spend the winter resting on trees in huge colonies. A colony may contain 100,000 butterflies or more.

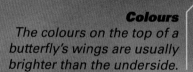

Colours
The colours on the top of a butterfly's wings are usually brighter than the underside.

EGGS
Most butterfly eggs are pale in colour and are laid on the underside of a leaf, so predators, such as birds, cannot see them.

*** This monarch egg** is on a milkweed plant.*

*A **larva**, or caterpillar, grows out of its skin several times as it grows. Monarch caterpillars eat only milkweed plants.*

Antennae
A butterfly's antennae are long and slender, ending with a 'club' shape. Moth antennae are usually thicker.

Mouthparts
An adult's mouthparts include the proboscis. This works like a drinking straw to soak and suck up nectar from inside a flower.

LIFE CYCLE

Like other butterflies and moths, monarchs have four stages to their life cycle: egg, larva, pupa and adult. The way that an insect changes from a larva to an adult is called metamorphosis.

PUPA

While a butterfly is a pupa, it is undergoing its metamorphosis. It stays in the chrysalis until it emerges as an adult.

A chrysalis protects the growing insect.

Males and females
Males and females look similar, but males are slightly larger than females and have dark spots on their wings.

FACT FILE

TYPE
Class: Insecta
Order: Lepidoptera

DIET
Plants, nectar

FOUND
Gardens, parks and woodlands of North America

0   10 cm

SIZE • 10 CM WINGSPAN

HAWKMOTHS

Hawkmoths are found in most regions of the world, but they are most common in warm places. There are more than 1000 species of hawkmoth and most of them are fast flyers. Hawkmoths visit gardens to feed on flower nectar and to lay their eggs.

Antennae
The sensitive antennae of hawkmoths are not as furry as those of other moths. Males have hairier antennae than females and they use them to find females by their smell.

FACT FILE

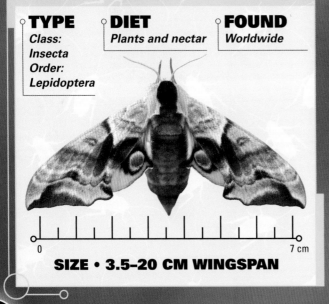

TYPE	DIET	FOUND
Class: Insecta Order: Lepidoptera	Plants and nectar	Worldwide

0   7 cm

SIZE • 3.5–20 CM WINGSPAN

⊕ LARVAE

Hawkmoths are large moths, and their larvae can grow to 10 centimetres long. The larvae feed on plants. Some of them are pests because they damage gardeners' food plants, such as tomato plants. They are called hornworms because they have a spike, or horn, at the end of the abdomen.

⊕ POLLINATORS

Like many insects, hawkmoths have an important job to do in the garden. They are pollinators: when they flit between flowers, they carry pollen with them. This fertilizes the flowers so fruits and seeds can grow.

Wings
The wings are long and elegant. Hawkmoths can reach speeds of 50 kph and migrate long distances.

HOVERING
Hawkmoths are superb flyers that can hover while they feed from a flower. They can also suddenly swoop to the side to avoid predators, such as birds.

When it hovers, the moth stays in one place.

FLOWER FEEDERS
Most garden moths are active at night. Hawkmoths can sometimes be seen in the day, often feeding on flowers, although they are more active in the mornings and evenings.

Insects are most active on warm, sunny days.

Eyespots
Butterflies and moths sometimes have bold patterns, called eyespots, on their wings. The insects flash their wings to reveal the eyespots and startle predators.

HONEYBEES

Busy garden bees visit plants, collecting nectar and pollen to eat. Most honeybees are worker females. They have pollen baskets on their legs to carry the food they harvest from flowers. In just one trip, a honeybee may visit up to 100 flowers before returning to the hive.

⊕ LIVING IN GROUPS

Bees are social insects. This means they live in large groups, called colonies, and they are divided into different types, or castes. Male bees are called drones, and their main job is to mate with the queen bee. There is one queen, whose job is to lay eggs. The other females make honey.

STINGER

A honeybee's stinger is barbed, so when it is pushed into flesh, it stays in place while the bee pumps venom into the wound. When the bee flies off, the stinger gets torn from the bee's body, causing the insect to die.

The stinger is at the tip of the bee's abdomen.

Legs
A honeybee has three pairs of legs. The hind legs have long, curved hairs that create the basket for carrying pollen.

THE NEST

Honeybees nest in tree hollows and in caves. In warm weather, the bees build their nest from wax made by the workers' bodies. The queen lays her eggs in these cells. When it turns cold, honey bees sleep through winter in the nest.

WORKER BEES

The worker bees look after the queen's eggs and young. They keep them clean and healthy, and even fan their wings to keep fresh air moving over the brood.

The grubs are first fed royal jelly (a food made by workers), then pollen and honey.

Wings
The two pairs of wings are attached to the thorax.

Eyes and antennae
Large eyes detect light, colour and movement. Sensitive antennae are used to sense smells and touch.

FACT FILE

TYPE
Class: Insecta
Order: Hymenoptera

DIET
Nectar and pollen

FOUND
Worldwide

0   15 mm

SIZE • 5–15 MM

Pollen sticks to the bee's hairs.

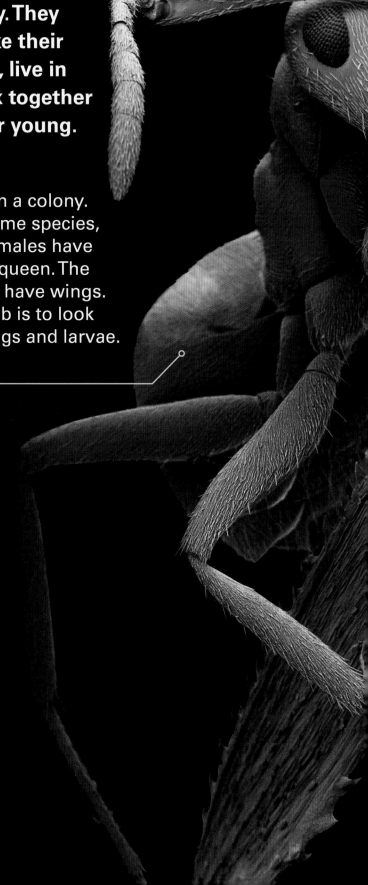

ANTS

Antennae
The antennae are bent, not straight. They are extremely sensitive to smells, and ants can follow each other's trails to a food source.

Of all the world's garden mini-beasts, ants are some of the most extraordinary. They may be small, but these insects, like their close relatives the bees and wasps, live in large groups, or colonies, and work together to build their homes and raise their young.

CASTES

There are three types, or castes, of ant in a colony. The queen's job is to lay eggs, and in some species, she lays a million eggs in a month. The males have wings, and their job is to mate with the queen. The worker ants are all females. They do not have wings. Workers never lay eggs because their job is to look after the colony and tend the queen's eggs and larvae.

Body shape
There are three distinct body parts: head, thorax and abdomen. The thorax and abdomen are separated by a narrow part, called the waist.

BITES AND STINGS

Ants are mostly harmless, but they can bite and sting. Bulldog and jumper ants bite their prey hard and then jab a sting, which is on the abdomen, into their victim's flesh.

An ant's sting contains formic acid.

 # ANT HOMES

Most ants live in the soil, where they build nests, dig burrows, bring food for the young and protect the queen.

Mouthparts
The shape and size of an ant's mouthparts depend on the species, caste, and what type of food it eats. Some ants have huge mandibles for crushing insects or slicing leaves.

USEFUL BUGS

Ants help to remove rotting plant matter and recycle the nutrients into the soil, keeping it fertile. However, they can also be pests and can destroy living trees.

Leafcutter ants cut and carry leaves.

ANTS AND APHIDS

Some garden ants look after aphids, protecting them from predators, so they can feed on the sweet liquid (honeydew) that the aphids make.

Ants create an 'aphid farm'.

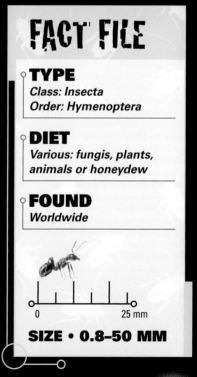 ## FACT FILE

TYPE
Class: Insecta
Order: Hymenoptera

DIET
Various: fungis, plants, animals or honeydew

FOUND
Worldwide

0   25 mm

SIZE • 0.8–50 MM

SPIDERS

Eyes
Most spiders have eight eyes, arranged in rows. Some spiders may be able to see colours, but not red.

Spiders are not insects; they are arachnids. Arachnids are an ancient group of invertebrates that also includes scorpions, ticks and mites. There are more than 40,000 species of spider and many of them live in gardens. They all spin silk and some use silk to build webs to trap their prey. Others hunt instead.

GARDEN HUNTERS

All spiders (except just one species) eat other animals, especially insects and other spiders. They are useful garden beasties because they help to control pests, and are food for birds and frogs.

Arachnid
An arachnid has two body segments: a head-thorax and an abdomen. Its four pairs of legs are attached to the head-thorax.

Legs
The legs can sense movement, touch, smell and even humidity (the amount of water in the air).

CRAB SPIDERS

Crab spiders are one of the most colourful spiders. They can mimic the colour of flowers, where they hide and wait for insects to come close. They leap at their prey, grabbing them before sinking their venomous jaws into them.

Spiders' legs are covered in hairs that are super-sensitive to movement. Their claws have tufts of hair that help them to stick to smooth surfaces, such as ceilings and walls.

FACT FILE

TYPE
Class: Arachnida
Order: Areneae

DIET
Insects, spiders and other small invertebrates

FOUND
Worldwide

0   30 mm

SIZE • 5–300 MM LEGSPAN

TICKS

Cats and dogs that stay outside often fall prey to blood-sucking ticks. These invertebrates belong to the same group as spiders, but they follow very different lifestyles. There are about 700 species of tick and they are found almost everywhere that mammals and birds live.

PARASITE

Ticks live on another animal, and they do it harm. Animals like this are called parasites, and the animals they harm are called their hosts. Garden ticks often attach themselves to pets, but they can also feed on humans.

Shield
A tick has a tough exoskeleton made up of plates. The one on its back is called a shield, or dorsal plate. The exoskeleton on its underside is softer so it can stretch during a blood meal.

Body shape
Ticks have two body parts: the head with mouthparts and the idiosoma, with the legs and digestive and reproductive systems.

FEEDING
The hypostome is barbed so that it sticks hard into the flesh and is very difficult to remove.

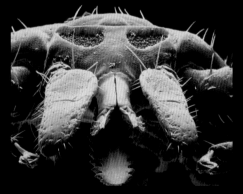

The mouth is in the centre, the palps are on either side.

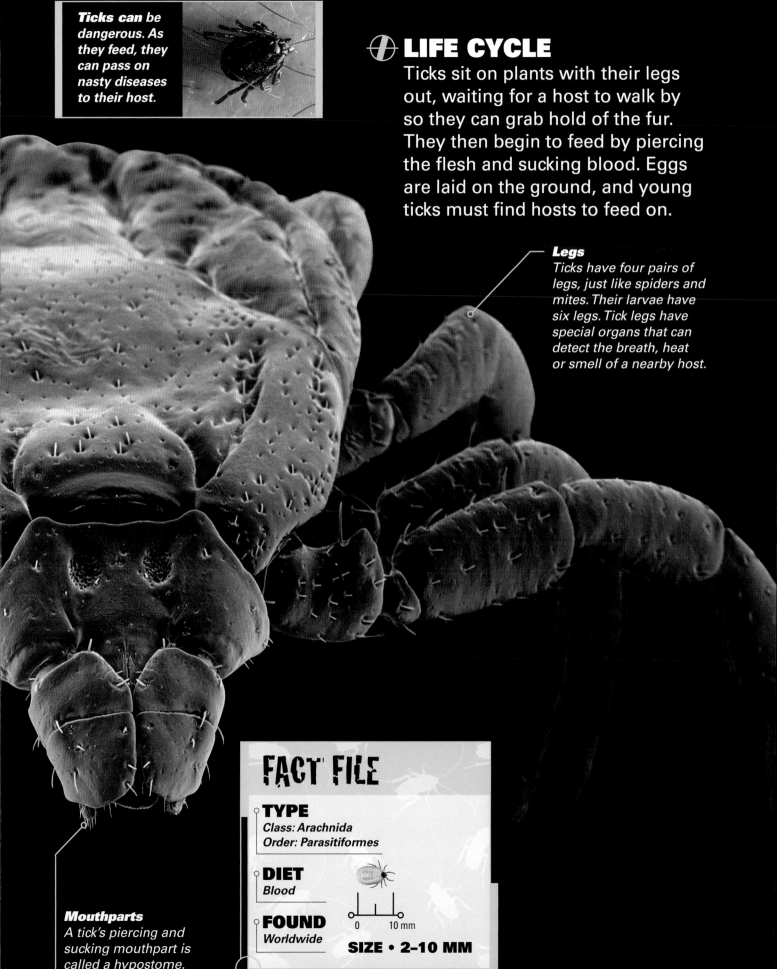

Ticks can be dangerous. As they feed, they can pass on nasty diseases to their host.

⊕ LIFE CYCLE

Ticks sit on plants with their legs out, waiting for a host to walk by so they can grab hold of the fur. They then begin to feed by piercing the flesh and sucking blood. Eggs are laid on the ground, and young ticks must find hosts to feed on.

Legs
Ticks have four pairs of legs, just like spiders and mites. Their larvae have six legs. Tick legs have special organs that can detect the breath, heat or smell of a nearby host.

Mouthparts
A tick's piercing and sucking mouthpart is called a hypostome.

FACT FILE

TYPE
Class: Arachnida
Order: Parasitiformes

DIET
Blood

FOUND
Worldwide

0   10 mm

SIZE • 2–10 MM

GLOSSARY

ABDOMEN
The hind part of an invertebrate's body that comes after the thorax.

ANTENNAE
A pair of sensitive feelers on the top or front of an invertebrate's head.

ANUS
The end of an animal's digestive system. This is where faeces or solid waste pass out of the body.

ARTHROPODS
Invertebrates that have exoskeletons and pairs of jointed legs. Spiders and insects are arthropods.

BACTERIA
Tiny living things that are made of just one cell.

CAMOUFLAGE
The way an animal can be coloured or patterned so it is hidden in its habitat.

COCOON
A silky case spun by some insects when they pupate.

COLONIES
Groups of animals that live together. Bees, ants and termites live in colonies.

COMPOST
Garden or food waste, such as fallen leaves or leftover vegetables, which is collected and left to rot. Eventually, it can be dug back into the soil to help new plants to grow.

COMPOUND EYES
Eyes made up of many lenses. Most insects have compound eyes, but humans have just one lens in each eye.

DUNG
Animal faeces or solid waste.

ENDANGERED
Describes a species of animal that is in danger of becoming extinct (dying out forever).

EXOSKELETON
An arthropod's tough outer skin.

GRUBS
Maggots, or larvae, especially of flies and beetles.

HABITAT
The place where an animal usually lives.

HIBERNATING
Spending the cold winter months in a state of deep rest, which is like sleep. Hibernating helps animals to survive a time when there is little food for them to eat.

INSECTS
Arthropods that have three distinct body segments – the head, thorax and abdomen. Insects also have three pairs of legs. Most insects have one or two pairs of wings.

INSTARS
Young invertebrates between moults.

INVERTEBRATES

Animals that do not have a backbone (spine). Animals that do have a spine are called vertebrates.

LARVAE

Young invertebrates. Many larvae look very different from the adults.

MANDIBLES

An arthropod's crushing or slicing mouthparts.

METAMORPHOSIS

The time when an insect changes from being a larva to an adult.

MOULTING

When an animal sheds its old skin, revealing its new skin beneath.

NECTAR

A sugary liquid made by flowers to attract insects and other invertebrates.

NOCTURNAL

Active at night.

NUTRIENTS

The goodness contained in a food. Nutrients are needed to live and grow.

NYMPHS

The young of some insects. Unlike larvae, nymphs often look like adults.

POLLEN

The yellow powder in a flower. Pollen fertilizes the eggs in a flower, so they can grow into seeds.

PREDATORS

Animals that hunt, kill and eat other animals.

PREY

An animal that is hunted, killed and eaten by other animals.

PROBOSCIS

The strawlike, sucking mouthpart used by some insects to feed.

PRONOTUM

A platelike structure on some insects. It covers the thorax, and often part of the head too. It protects the insect, like armour.

PUPATE

When an insect is changing from larva to adult, it is said to pupate. When it is a pupa, the insect is protected in a leathery case.

SAP

A sugary liquid that moves through the inside of a plant.

THORAX

The middle segment of an insect's body. Wings and legs are attached to the thorax.

TRANSPARENT

See-through.

TROPICAL

The areas that are found around the Equator, between the Tropic of Cancer and the Tropic of Capricorn. A tropical climate is usually very warm, with plenty of rain, all year round.

VENOM

A poison made in an animal's body and used to injure or kill another animal.

WINGSPAN

The measurement from one wing tip to another, across an animal's body.

INDEX

ACKNOWLEDGMENTS

Picture credits

(t=top, b=bottom, l=left, r=right, c=centre, fc=front cover)

Alamy 14–15 blickwinkel, 60–61 imageBROKER

FLPA 69tr Roger Tidman

Nature PL 3tl Fabrice Cahez, 33br Visuals Unlimited, 33tl Visuals Unlimited, 37br Fabrice Cahez, 39bl Kim Taylor, 42bl Nature Production

Science Photo Library 1b Eye of Science, 3tr Power and Syred, 4 Power and Syred, 6tr David Aubrey, 6bl Frank Fox, 8b Power and Syred, 8–9 Steve Gschmeissner, 9br Eye of Science, 9cr Steve Gschmeissner, 9tr Power and Syred, 10–11 Colin Varndell, 11br Colin Varndell, 11c Ian Gowland, 12bl Power and Syred, 12–13 Colin Varndell, 13c Gregory S. Paulson, 14br Clouds Hill Imaging Ltd, 15bl Alex Hyde, 15tr Natural History Museum, London, 16–17 Paul Whitten, 17bl John Serrao, 17c Sheri Neva/ Cultura, 18c Steve Gschmeissner, 20l Fabio Pupin/Visuals Unlimited, 21tl Steve Gschmeissner, 25tr Scott Camazine, 27br David Scharf, 28–29 Nicholas Reusens, 29tr Thierry Berrod, Mona Lisa Production, 30bl Eye of Science, 30–31 Clouds Hill Imaging Ltd, 31bl Dr Jeremy Burgess, 31cl Power and Syred, 32tr A Cosmos Blank, 32–33 Gilles Mermet, 34br Dr John Brackenbury, 34–35 Power and Syred, 35br Steve Gschmeissner, 35tr Power and Syred, 36cl Dr John Brackenbury, 37bl Dr Jeremy Burgess, 42–43 Steve Gschmeissner, 44–45 Power and Syred, 46tr F. Martinez Clavel, 47cr F. Martinez Clavel, 47tr Claude Nuridsany and Marie Perennou, 48cl Martin Shields, 49br Nicholas Reusens, 50bl Georgette Douwma, 51cr Natural History Museum, London, 52tl Eye of Science, 52–53 David Scharf, 53br Dr David Wheeler, 53tr David Scharf, 54–55 Philippe Psaila, 55br Thomas Shahan, 55tr Thomas Shahan, 56bl Steve Gschmeissner, 57br David Parker, 58br Larry West, 58–59 Dr Fred Hossler/Visuals Unlimited Inc, 59tr Martin Dohrn, 60tl Nigel Cattlin, 61tr Clouds Hill Imaging Ltd, 62cl Steve Percival, 62–63 Terry Priest/Visuals Unlimited Inc, 63bl Jeff Daly/Visuals Unlimited Inc, 63cr Jeff Daly/Visuals Unlimited Inc, 63tr Steve Gschmeissner, 64bl Edward Kinsman, 64br Richard S Trump, 64–65 Frans Lanting, Mint Images, 65tr Frans Lanting, Mint Images, 68bl Steve Gschmeissner, 68–69 Dr Jeremy Burgess, 69br Susumu Nishinaga, 70bl B.G. Thomson, 70–71 Eye of Science, 73tl Susumu Nishinaga, 74bl Eye of Science, 74–75 Eye of Science, 75bl Nigel Cattlin, 75tl Fabio Pupin/Visuals Unlimited

Shutterstock: 1tl irin-k, 1tr irin-k, 03bl Lightspring, 03br smuay, 05yanikap, 06–7 reptiles4all, 10bl Sanit Fuangnakhon, 11tr Erni, 13br Scott Sanders, 13tl KOO, 14c irin-k, 16br Vitalii Hulai, 17tr yanikap, 18bc evantravels, 18br Eric Isselee, 18–19 Tyler Fox, 19br Katarina Christenson, 20br Awei, 20–21 Tomatito, 21br Henrik Larsson, 22br Ratchapol Yindeesuk, 22–23 Lakeview Images, 23br Eric Isselee, 23c Andrew Burgess, 23tl D. Kucharski K. Kucharska, 24tr Cathy Keifer, 24–25 Greir, 25c Eric Isselee, 26bl Preecha Ngamsrisan, 26–27 seeyou, 27cr smuay, 27tr natrot, 28bl Stanislav Fosenbauer, 29br Dr. Morley Read, 29tl skynetphoto, 31tr Henrik Larsson, 34cl claffra, 36–37 Steve Byland, 37cr alexisvirid, 38br skynetphoto, 38–39 Lukas Hejtman, 39br MarkMirror, 39cr Lukas Hejtman, 40cl Kingfisher, 40cr Andrey Burmakin, 40–41 claffra, 41br Anton Kozyrev, 41tr Paul Looyen, 43bl David Lee, 43cr Chris Moody, 43tr Mauro Rodrigues, 44bl symbiot, 45bl Subbotina Anna, 45cr PHOTO FUN, 45tr Akil Rolle-Rowan, 46bl Seksan44, 46–47 Pukhouskaya Ina, 47br CreativeNature R.Zwerver, 48br Jiri Hodecek, 48–49 mrfiza, 49tr Henrik Larsson, 50bl Digoarpi, 50–51 alslutsky, 51br Sakdinon Kadchiangsaen, 55cr Pan Xunbin, 56–57 paulrommer, 57tr paulrommer, 58cl Kletr, 59br Thanapun, 61bl paulrommer, 61br alexsvirid, 65tr Lightspring, 66bl Tatsiana_S, 66–67 Tatsiana_S, 67cr Cristian Gusa, 67tr Cristian Gusa, 69cr irin-k, 71bl Radu Bercan, 71br Andrey Pavlov, 71cr Ryan M. Bolton, 72–73 Tomatito, 73tr Eric Isselee, 76 Eric Isselee, 78 Anton Kozyrev, 79 KOO